MIND BENDERS® B4

DEDUCTIVE THINKING S[...]

SERIES TITLES

Mind Benders® Warm Up, Mind Benders® A1, Mind Benders® A2, Mind Benders® A3, Mind Benders® A4, Mind Benders® B1, Mind Benders® B2, Mind Benders® B3, Mind Benders® B4, Mind Benders® C1, Mind Benders® C2, Mind Benders® C3

ANITA HARNADEK

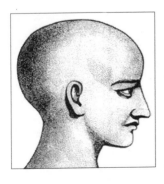

© 2000, 1981
CRITICAL THINKING BOOKS & SOFTWARE
www.CriticalThinking.com
P.O. Box 448 • Pacific Grove • CA 93950-0448
Phone 800-458-4849 • FAX 831-393-3277
ISBN 0-89455-127-2
Printed in the United States of America

TABLE OF CONTENTS

TEACHER SUGGESTIONS

PURPOSE

Students having wide ranges of ability, motivation, and achievement seem to be remarkably attracted to Mind Benders® problems. Students who may or may not try to use deductive reasoning for ordinary classwork or homework seem to think Mind Benders® are fun, not work. So the purpose of the MIND BENDERS® series is to give each student what (s)he wants—fun, a happy diversion from routine—while at the same time forcing the student to organize sets of clues—some direct, some indirect—and reach logical conclusions by using pure deductive reasoning.

GENERAL INFORMATION

There are twelve exercise books in this series:

WARM-UP MIND BENDERS®

MIND BENDERS® A1

MIND BENDERS® A2

MIND BENDERS® A3

MIND BENDERS® A4

MIND BENDERS® B1

MIND BENDERS® B2

MIND BENDERS® B3

MIND BENDERS® B4

MIND BENDERS® C1

MIND BENDERS® C2

MIND BENDERS® C3

The **A** series is easy, **B** is medium, and **C** is hard.

Although most of the problems in WARM UP MIND BENDERS® vary from extremely easy to easy, there are a handful in the medium range. The idea of the problems in the warmup book is to give the students practice in using deductive reasoning in very simple situations before presenting them with more clues to use and with clues which are more subtle, as in the other MIND BENDERS® books.

Since some teachers will need more problems for their students than other teachers, more than one book is available in each of the A, B, and C categories. Within a category, there is no substantial difference in difficulty between the books offered. (For example, a teacher who needs only 15 problems at the easy level may order any of the four MIND BENDERS® books in the A series.)

See page iv for general comments about assumptions that can be made from clues.

HELPFUL HINTS ABOUT SOLVING MIND BENDERS®

Most Mind Benders® in the A, B, and C categories are solved more easily if a chart is used than if the solver simply makes notes about the clues given. To help students solve the problems, each Mind Bender® is accompanied by a chart made especially for that particular problem.

See page vi for a step-by-step explanation of using charts to solve Mind Bender® problems, including the way each chart looks after each step. None of the problems used there are used as exercises in any of the MIND BENDERS® books.

The instructions (in highly abbreviated form, of course) are these: To fill in a chart, make a notation in each square which is eliminated by a clue. (The notation might be the clue number or the word "no," for example.) When there is only one blank square left in a row (or column) within a category, then "X" that square. Then note the elimination of all the other squares in the matching column (or row). When a chart contains three or more categories, then either the elimination of a square or the "X"ing of a square may also give you more information about previous clues. (For example, if you know that Mr. Brown owns the red car and you have just discovered that the Chevrolet is not the red car, then you have also discovered that Mr. Brown does not own the Chevrolet.)

SOLUTIONS

Note 1: Each problem has only one solution. If the notation used for eliminations is simply a "no," then the completed chart will have an "X" for each combination named in the solutions given below, and the chart will have a "no" everywhere else. If the notation used for elimination is a clue number, however, then the completed chart may vary from one student to another. (This is because eliminations can sometimes be made in different orders.)

Note 2: If your solutions do not agree with those given, refer to the Examples and Step-by-Step Procedures on page vi for information on how to use charts to solve Mind Benders® problems.

About the Clues in MIND BENDERS®

In general, the MIND BENDERS® assume that you will, when using the clues, apply three guidelines unless a problem leads you to believe otherwise:

1. Think of everyday situations rather than of highly unusual exceptions.

2. Think of standards which are generally acceptable to U.S. society as a whole.

3. Use common sense and context in deciding what the clues mean.

Following are examples:

a. Assume that only males have male names (John, Robert, Dave) and only females have female names (Mary, Jennifer, Cathy). But be careful not to make such assumptions about unisex names (Pat, Chris).

b. Assume that typical U.S. social relationships apply. For example, if John is engaged to Mary, you may assume they know each other. You may assume that very close relatives know each other.

c. Don't assume that rare age relationships may apply. For example, don't assume that a 7 year old might be a college graduate, or that a parent might be younger than his or her adopted child. On the other hand, although most cases of age may be in one direction, enough cases in the other direction may exist so that these would not be considered especially unusual. For example, a husband may be a good deal younger than his wife, or a 45 year old may get the mumps.

d. Assume that animals are of normal size. For example, "a horse" is not "a pygmy horse"; "a small dog" is smaller than a goat; a "large dog" is simply one of the larger breeds of dogs. If a problem talks about a cat and a fox, assume that the cat is smaller than the fox. Do not think that maybe the cat is fully grown and the fox is a few weeks old.

e. Assume that animals are called by their usual names within the context. For example, if John and Mary have a pet dog and a pet cat, assume that the cat is an ordinary household cat, rather than maybe a tiger or a leopard.

f. Don't look for tricky situations. For example, suppose the problem has four houses in a row (and no other houses). And suppose Debby lives next door to Gary. Don't assume that Debby or Gary might live in a garage between two of the houses. That is, assume that they live in two of the four houses in the problem.

g. Assume that typical U.S. social situations apply. For example, if John went on a date with Abbott, assume two things: (1) Abbott is a female; (2) neither John nor Abbott is married, since (a) when a married couple go out, we do not call it a "date," and (b) if either one is married to someone else, then it is not typical for him or her to be dating someone.

h. Pay attention to what the clues say. For example, suppose a problem has four people, and suppose one clue says, "Cathy and the dentist ride to work together in a car pool." Also suppose another clue says, "Brown, who does not know any of the other three people, is not the typist." Then you should deduce that neither Cathy nor the dentist is Brown.

i. Exact wording to eliminate ambiguities sometimes makes a clue too long. The clue is then shortened to the point where it is unambiguous to most people, but some people would still recognize ambiguities and object to the wording. In such cases, consider the context and the intent of the clue. As examples:

   (1) "Neither Bob nor Young lives in the white house," means, "Bob is not Young, and Bob does not live in the white house, and Young does not live in the white house."

   (2) "John and Abbott went bowling with Dave and Smith," means, "Four different people went bowling together. One of these was John, one was Abbott, one was Dave, and one was Smith."

   (3) "Jane doesn't know either Mary or the artist," means, "Jane doesn't know Mary, and Jane doesn't know the artist, and Mary is not the artist."

   (4) "Neither Carol nor Bill went to the party, and Norris didn't go, either," refers to three different people.

(5) In general, "neither ... nor" and "either ... or" sentences will refer to separate things, as in the above examples. Just plain "or" sentences, however, are sometimes less definite, as in this example: "Neither Becky nor Jackson has the dog or is the secretary." Here, Becky and Jackson are different people, but we aren't sure that the person who has the dog is not also the secretary.

MISCELLANEOUS INFORMATION

Most of the problems you will find that are similar to these Mind Benders® seem to be good ones, but you may run into some that could be better. Here are examples of clues from such problems:

1. One clue reads, "Abbott told Baker that he could beat her at weight lifting." You can't tell which one is the man and which is the woman from this sentence. It may be that a man (Abbott) is claiming that he can beat a woman (Baker) at weight lifting, or it may be that a woman (Abbott) is claiming that a man (Baker) can beat her at weight lifting.

2. One clue tells you that Abbott is single, and another clue refers to John's children. You don't know whether or not the writer thinks that single people don't have children. (Maybe he adopted children.)

3. Some problems have contradictory clues. I once saw a problem in which one clue said that Abbott spent all of his spare time doing one thing (reading, for example), and another clue said that John was doing something else with his friends (watching TV, for example). So I marked on the chart that John was not Abbott. But a few minutes later I found the problem to be unsolvable, so I looked at the solution which came with it. The solution showed that John was Abbott.

EXAMPLES AND STEP-BY-STEP PROCEDURES

A Mind Bender® problem gives you two or more lists of things and asks you to match each item in one list with an item in the other list. Finding answers is easier if a chart is made showing all the lists at once and is then filled in. Note that the number of small boxes (within one large box) is the square of the number of things in any one list. (Example 1 has three things in each list, so each large box has 9 small boxes).

THREE-DIMENSIONAL PROBLEMS

To solve a three-dimensional problem, we make the chart so that each item in each list can be compared with each item in both other lists.

EXAMPLE 1

Problem: Davis, Edwards, and Farman are an astronaut, a bookbinder, and a skin diver. Their ages are 25, 30, and 35. Match each person's name, job, and age.

1. Davis is younger than the astronaut but older than Farman.

2. The skin diver is younger than the bookbinder.

Solution: To help keep our thinking straight on clue 1, we'll write in mathematical symbols: $F < D < A$. Then Farman is the youngest, Davis is in the middle, and the astronaut is the oldest. So Farman is 25, Davis is 30, and the astronaut is 35.

It is important to notice here that if the puzzle involved four people instead of three, we could not say that Farman is the youngest or that the astronaut is the oldest. The most we could say is (1) Farman is not either of the two oldest people, (2) Davis is not either the oldest or the youngest person, and (3) the astronaut is not either of the two youngest people. Let's look at how the chart works for this kind of problem.

Clue 1, step 1

	A	B	SD	25	30	35
D	1				X	
E						
F	1			X		
25						
30						
35	X					

Clue 1, step 2

	A	B	SD	25	30	35
D	1			25	X	D
E				25	30	
F	1			X	F	F
25	A					
30	A					
35	X	35	35			

Clue 1, step 3

	A	B	SD	25	30	35
D	1			25	X	D
E	X	E	E	25	30	X
F	1			X	F	F
25	A					
30	A					
35	X	35	35			

Clue 2 says the skin diver is younger than the bookbinder. The chart (from *clue 1, step 3*) says that Edwards, the astronaut, is 35. This leaves ages 25 and 30. So the skin diver is 25 and the bookbinder is 30. But we know from the chart that Farman is 25 and Davis is 30. So Farman is the skin diver and Davis is the bookbinder.

Solution: Davis, bookbinder, 30; Edwards, astronaut, 35; Farman, skin diver, 25.

	A	B	SD	25	30	35
D	1	X	SD	25	X	D
E	X	E	E	25	30	X
F	1	F	X	X	F	F
25	A	25	X			
30	A	X	SD			
35	X	35	35			

EXAMPLE 2

Problem: Davis, Edwards, Farman, and Gurley are an astronaut, a bookbinder, a plumber, and a skin diver. Their first names are Harold, Jenny, Ken, and Laura. Match up each person's full name and job.

1. Farman and the astronaut joined the same fraternity in college.

2. Edwards said she'd teach Jenny how to swim.

3. Ken asked the plumber if he could install a solar heating system for him.

4. Davis enjoys her work.

Solution: (Can you solve this one before reading the solution below?)

Clue 1

M₁ (over F), M₁ (over A)

		D	E	F	G	A	B	P	SD
M	H								
F	J			FM		FM			
M	K								
F	L			FM		FM			
M₁	A			1					
	B								
	P								
	SD								

Clue 2

F₂ (over E), M₁ (over F), M₁ (over A)

		D	E	F	G	A	B	P	SD
M	H		MF						
F	J		2	FM		FM			2
M	K		MF						
F	L	L	X	FM	L	FM			
M₁	A		MF	1					
	B								
	P								
	SD								

Clue 3, step 1

F₂ (over E), M₁ (over F), M₁ (over A), M₃ (over P)

		D	E	F	G	A	B	P	SD
M	H		MF			H	H	X	H
F	J		2	FM		FM		FM	2
M	K		MF					3	
F	L	L	X	FM	L	FM		FM	
M₁	A		MF	1					
	B								
M₃	P		MF						
	SD								

Clue 3, step 2

Group headers: F₂ (over E) · M₁ (over F–G) · M₁ (over A–B) · M₃ (over P–SD)

		D	E	F	G	A	B	P	SD
M	H		MF			H	H	X	H
F	J		2	FM		FM		FM	2
M	K		MF			X	K	3	K
F	L	L	X	FM	L	FM		FM	
M₁	A		MF	1					
	B								
M₃	P		MF						
	SD								

Clue 3, step 3*

		D	E	F	G	A	B	P	SD
M	H		MF			H	H	X	H
F	J		2	FM		FM		FM	2
M	K		MF	3,1*		X	K	3	K
F	L	L	X	FM	L	FM		FM	
M₁	A		MF	1					
	B								
M₃	P		MF						
	SD								

*The "F" column says Farman is not the astronaut *(clue 1)*. But step 2 of *clue 3* says Ken is the astronaut. Therefore, Ken is not Farman.

Clue 3, step 4

		D	E	F	G	A	B	P	SD
M	H		MF			H	H	X	H
F	J		2	FM		FM	X	FM	2
M	K		MF	3,1		X	K	3	K
F	L	L	X	FM	L	FM	B	FM	X
M₁	A		MF	1					
	B								
M₃	P		MF						
	SD								

Clue 3, step 5

		D	E	F	G	A	B	P	SD
M	H	H	MF	X	H	H	H	X	H
F	J		2	FM		FM	X	FM	2
M	K		MF	3,1		X	K	3	K
F	L	L	X	FM	L	FM	B	FM	X
M₁	A		MF	1					
	B								
M₃	P		MF						
	SD								

Clue 3, step 6

		D	E	F	G	A	B	P	SD
M	H	H	MF	X	H	H	H	X	H
F	J		2	FM		FM	X	FM	2
M	K		MF	3,1		X	K	3	K
F	L	L	X	FM	L	FM	B	FM	X
M₁	A		MF	1					
	B			F					
M₃	P	P	MF	X	P				
	SD			F					

Clue 3, step 7

		D	E	F	G	A	B	P	SD
M	H	H	MF	X	H	H	H	X	H
F	J		2	FM		FM	X	FM	2
M	K		MF	3,1		X	K	3	K
F	L	L	X	FM	L	FM	B	FM	X
M₁	A		MF	1					
	B		E	F					
M₃	P	P	MF	X	P				
	SD	SD	X	F	SD				

Clue 4, step 1

Group headers: F₄ · F₂ · M₁ · M₁ · M₃

		F₄	D	E	F	G	A	B	P	SD
M	H		H	MF	X	H	H	H	X	H
F	J	X		2	FM	J	FM	X	FM	2
M	K	MF		MF	3,1		X	K	3	K
F	L	L		X	FM	L	FM	B	FM	X
M₁	A			MF	1					
	B			E	F					
M₃	P	P		MF	X	P				
	SD	SD		X	F	SD				

Clue 4, step 2

		F₄	D	E	F	G	A	B	P	SD
M	H		H	MF	X	H	H	H	X	H
F	J	X		2	FM	J	FM	X	FM	2
M	K	MF		MF	3,1		X	K	3	K
F	L	L		X	FM	L	FM	B	FM	X
M₁	A		D	MF	1					
	B	X		E	F	B				
M₃	P	P		MF	X	P				
	SD	SD		X	F	SD				

Clue 4, step 3

		F₄	D	E	F	G	A	B	P	SD
M	H		H	MF	X	H	H	H	X	H
F	J	X		2	FM	J	FM	X	FM	2
M	K	MF		MF	3,1		X	X	K	3	K
F	L	L		X	FM	L	FM	B	FM	X
M₁	A		D	MF	1	X				
	B	X		E	F	B				
M₃	P	P		MF	X	P				
	SD	SD		X	F	SD				

The solution is this: Harold Farman, plumber; Jenny Davis, bookbinder; Ken Gurley, astronaut; Laura Edwards, skin diver

Here's one more three-dimensional puzzle for you to try before we go on to a four-dimensional puzzle.

EXAMPLE 3

Problem: Harold, Jenny, Ken, and Laura are 12, 16, 20, and 25 years old. Their last names are Davis, Edwards, Farman, and Gurley. Find each person's full name and age.

1. Harold's and Gurley's ages are perfect squares.

2. Edwards is Jenny's older sister.

3. Farman is younger than Ken but older than Edwards' sister.

Solution: *Clue 1*: (a) Harold is not Gurley. (b) The only perfect squares listed are 16 and 25, so neither Harold nor Gurley is 12 or 20.

Clue 1

		D	E	F	G	12	16	20	25
M	H			1	1			1	
F	J								
M	K								
F	L								
	12			1					
	16								
	20			1					
	25								

Clue 2, step 1: (a) Edwards is a female and is not Jenny. So Edwards is Laura. (b) From *clue 1*, the ages of 16 and 25 are taken by Ken and Gurley, and Laura Edwards is neither of these people. So she is either 12 or 20. But she is older than Jenny, so she cannot be the youngest person, 12. So Laura Edwards is 20.

Clue 2, step 1

		D	E (F_2)	F	G	12	16	20 (F_2)	25
M	H		MF		1	1		1	
F	J		2					20	
M	K		MF					20	
F	L	L	X	L	L	2	2,1	X	2,1
	12		2		1				
	16		2,1						
F_2	20	20	X	20	1				
	25		2,1						

Clue 2, step 2: (a) Laura Edwards is 20 and is older than Jenny, so Jenny is either 12 or 16. (b) So neither Jenny nor Laura is 25. Then the 25 year old is a male.

Clue 2, step 2

		D	E (F_2)	F	G	12	16	20 (F_2)	25 (M_2)
M	H		MF		1	1		1	
F	J		2					20	2
M	K		MF					20	
F	L	L	X	L	L	2	2,1	X	2,1
	12		2		1				
	16		2,1						
F_2	20	20	X	20	1				
M_2	25		2,1						

Clue 3, step 1: Edwards' sister is Jenny *(clue 2)*, so Farman is younger than Ken but older than Jenny. In mathematical notation, $J < F < K$. Laura Edwards, 20, is not Jenny or Farman or Ken, so the only ages left are 12, 16 and 25. So Jenny is 12, Farman is 16, and Ken is 25.

Clue 3, step 1

		D	E	F	G	12	16	20	25
M	H		MF		1	1		1	25
F	J		2			X	J	20	2
M	K		MF			12	K	20	X
F	L	L	X	L	L	2	2,1	X	2,1
	12		2	F	1				
	16	16	2,1	X	16				
F_2	20	20	X	20	1				
M_2	25		2,1	F					

Clue 3, step 2: We look for remaining spaces we are forced to X, and we X them.

Clue 3, step 2

		D	E	F	G	12	16	20	25
M	H		MF		1	1	X	1	25
F	J		2			X	J	20	2
M	K		MF			12	K	20	X
F	L	L	X	L	L	2	2,1	X	2,1
	12	X	2	F	1				
	16	16	2,1	X	16				
F_2	20	20	X	20	1				
M_2	25	D	2,1	F	X				

Clue 3, step 3: (a) The chart shows that Harold and Farman are both 16, so Harold is Farman. (b) Jenny and Davis are both 12, so Jenny is Davis. (c) Only the K/G space is left. Since Ken and Gurley are both 25, we X this space.

So the solution is this: Harold Farman, 16; Jenny Davis, 12; Ken Gurley, 25; Laura Edwards, 20.

Clue 3, step 3

		D	E	F	G	12	16	20	25
M	H	H	MF	X	1	1	X	1	25
F	J	X	2	F	J	X	J	20	2
M	K	D	MF	F	X	12	K	20	X
F	L	L	X	L	L	2	2,1	X	2,1
	12	X	2	F	1				
	16	16	2,1	X	16				
F_2	20	20	X	20	1				
M_2	25	D	2,1	F	X				

FOUR- AND FIVE-DIMENSIONAL PROBLEMS

A problem of four or more dimensions is solved the same way as the others. Again, the chart must be made so that each list can be compared with all the other lists.

EXAMPLE 4

Problem: Davis, Edwards, and Gurley are the first, second, and third basemen for the Detroit Tigers. Their first names are Harold, José, and Ken. Their ages are 23, 25, and 28. From the clues below, match up everything.

1. The second baseman has a higher batting average than Ken or Davis.

2. The first baseman is younger than Edwards and older than Ken.

3. José and Davis ate pizza with some of the rest of the team after yesterday's game.

Solution:

Clue 1

	D	E	G	1st	2nd	3rd	23	25	28
H									
J									
K	1				1				
1st									
2nd	1								
3rd									
23									
25									
28									

Clue 2, step 1

(K < 1st < E)

	D	E	G	1st	2nd	3rd	23	25	28
H			G			3rd	23		
J			G			3rd	23		
K	1	2	X	2	1	X	X	2	2
1st		2							
2nd	1								
3rd									
23		2		2					
25		2		X	25	25			
28	28	X		28	2				

Clue 2, step 2 (Gurley is Ken, so post facts about Ken in Gurley's column. Also match "3rd" and "23.")

	D	E	G	1st	2nd	3rd	23	25	28
H			G			3rd	23		
J			G			3rd	23		
K	1	2	X	2	1	X	X	2	2
1st		2	K						
2nd	1		K						
3rd	3rd	3rd	X						
23	23	2	X	2	23	X			
25		2	K	X	25	25			
28	28	X	28	2		3rd			

Clue 2, step 3

	D	E	G	1st	2nd	3rd	23	25	28
H			G			3rd	23		
J			G			3rd	23		
K	1	2	X	2	1	X	X	2	2
1st	X	2	K						
2nd	1	X	K						
3rd	3rd	3rd	X						
23	23	2	X	2	23	X			
25	X	2	K	X	25	25			
28	28	X	28	2	X	3rd			

Clue 3, step 1

	D	E	G	1st	2nd	3rd	23	25	28
H	X	H	G			3rd	23		
J	3	X	G			3rd	23		
K	1	2	X	2	1	X	X	2	2
1st	X	2	K						
2nd	1	X	K						
3rd	3rd	3rd	X						
23	23	2	X	2	23	X			
25	X	2	K	X	25	25			
28	28	X	28	2	X	3rd			

The rest of the entries are now forced, so the chart is left for you to complete.

The solution is this: Harold Davis, first baseman, 25; José Edwards, second baseman, 28; Ken Gurley, third baseman, 23.

The preceding problem gave us four lists of things to match up (first names, last names, positions, and ages), and so is called a four-dimensional problem. A general chart for a four-dimensional problem would look like the one at the right.

	headings for second list	headings for third list	headings for fourth list
headings for first list	small boxes	small boxes	small boxes
headings for third list	small boxes		
headings for fourth list	small boxes	small boxes	

A chart for a five-dimensional problem (a problem with five lists of things to match up) would look like the one at the right.

	headings for second list	headings for third list	headings for fourth list	headings for fifth list
headings for first list	small boxes	small boxes	small boxes	small boxes
headings for third list	small boxes			
headings for fourth list	small boxes	small boxes		
headings for fifth list	small boxes	small boxes	small boxes	

EXERCISES
Clues and Charts

1. Teacher's Pens

Four teachers (Corwin, Dalton, Ephraim, Fenner) use four different colors of pen (black, blue, green, red) to correct the papers of their students. The teachers' first names are Jim, Mary, Stella, and Tom.

Match up everything from the clues below.

1. Corwin and Ephraim are to be bridesmaids at a wedding next week.

2. The teacher who uses the green pen rode to school with Mary in her car when his car was being repaired yesterday.

3. Jim always walks to school, but Ephraim always takes a bus to school.

4. Corwin told the teacher who uses a black pen that Fenner, who doesn't use a green pen, is an excellent teacher.

5. The teacher who uses the red pen lost his watch two days ago.

Chart for Problem 1

	Corwin	Dalton	Ephraim	Fenner	black	blue	green	red
Jim								
Mary								
Stella								
Tom								
black								
blue								
green								
red								

2. Building a House

The Smiths built a brick ranch-style home with a basement of poured concrete. Among the contractors they hired were a carpenter, an electrician, a mason, and a plumber. Their names are Norton, Otis, Robbins, and Taylor. The first names of the contractors are Andrew, Betty, Donna, and Jerome.

Read the clues below and match up everything.

1. Andrew and Taylor both finished their jobs before Otis started on his.

2. Neither Betty nor Taylor is the electrician.

3. Betty is not the mason.

4. Robbins is Norton's sister.

5. Donna is not the carpenter.

Chart for Problem 2

	Norton	Otis	Robbins	Taylor	carpenter	electrician	mason	plumber
Andrew								
Betty								
Donna								
Jerome								
carpenter								
electrician								
mason								
plumber								

3. Birthday Party

Sharon had a birthday party, and among her friends who attended were Angela, Carlotta, Elias, Harold, and Igor, whose last names are Durwood, Forman, Kramer, Lansdowne, and Nardon. The gifts they gave Sharon were a book, a game, a jigsaw puzzle, a model airplane kit, and a record album.

Match up everything from the clues below.

1. Elias didn't give Sharon a record album.

2. One of the girls thought Igor was kind of strange for giving Sharon a model airplane kit, but Sharon said she'd wanted one for a long time.

3. Durwood asked Nardon if he thought Sharon liked the gift she gave, which was not a game.

4. Forman was pleased by Sharon's smile when she saw his gift.

5. The girl who gave Sharon the book, who is not Angela, asked Kramer if he'd read it.

6. Igor and Forman started to put Nardon's gift together, but Nardon and Sharon made them stop.

7. A girl gave Sharon the game.

Chart for Problem 3

	Durwood	Forman	Kramer	Lans-downe	Nardon	book	game	jigsaw puzzle	model airplane	record album
Angela										
Carlotta										
Elias										
Harold										
Igor										
book										
game										
jigsaw puzzle										
model airplane										
record album										

4. Hair Colors

The hair colors of Catherine, Duane, Elias, Harmony, and Jane, whose last names are Fernandez, Inwell, Klinger, Lopez, and Mason, are auburn, black, gray, red, and yellow.

Match up everything from the clues below.

1. Duane, who does not dye his naturally blond hair, asked Mason if her curly hair was natural.

2. Jane and Mason kid Lopez about his long eyelashes and curly hair, which is not yellow.

3. Catherine, whose hair is straight, is not Klinger.

4. The person with auburn hair asked Fernandez and Duane if they'd like to play tennis with Harmony and her tomorrow.

5. Mason's hair is not gray or red.

6. Jane's hair doesn't have any reddish colors in it.

Chart for Problem 4

	Fernandez	Inwell	Klinger	Lopez	Mason	auburn	black	gray	red	yellow
Catherine										
Duane										
Elias										
Harmony										
Jane										
auburn										
black										
gray										
red										
yellow										

5. Fairy Tales

Four parents (Alice, Carlos, Kathleen, Paul) read stories ("Beauty and the Beast," "Hansel and Gretel," "Red Riding Hood," "Snow White") to their children (Fernando, Isabelle, Monica, Thomas). Their last names are Dorman, Ellman, Garner, and Jarvis.

Read the clues below and match up everything.

1. The men read to girls.

2. The stories Alice and Jarvis read did not have colors in their titles.

3. Garner did not read "Hansel and Gretel" to her child.

4. Jarvis' child is not Isabelle or Monica.

5. Isabelle, whose parent is not Paul, did not have "Red Riding Hood" read to her.

6. "Snow White" was not read to Dorman's child.

7. "Beauty and the Beast" was not read to Fernando.

Chart for Problem 5

	Dorman	Ellman	Garner	Jarvis	Fernando	Isabelle	Monica	Thomas	Beauty and the Beast	Hansel and Gretel	Red Riding Hood	Snow White
Alice												
Carlos												
Kathleen												
Paul												
Fernando												
Isabelle												
Monica												
Thomas												
Beauty and the Beast												
Hansel and Gretel												
Red Riding Hood												
Snow White												

6. Picnic in the Park

Four married couples (Creightons, Farmers, Garsons, Ordways) met in the park for a potluck picnic. They took apple pie, bean salad, iced tea, and potato salad (one item per couple). The husbands' first names are Brad, Edward, Homer, and Ken. The wives' first names are Daphne, Lisa, Moira, and Norma.

Match up everything from the clues below.

1. Brad and his wife, who didn't take iced tea, rode to the picnic with the Ordways, who didn't take apple pie, in their car.

2. Moira and her husband went to the picnic on their motorcycles.

3. The Farmers went to the picnic on their bicycles.

4. The Creightons didn't go to the picnic in a car.

5. Homer and Mrs. Farmer went swimming while Mr. Farmer and Edward played horseshoes with Lisa and Daphne.

6. Edward, who didn't go to the picnic in a car, did not take apple pie or bean salad.

7. Brad, who isn't married to Daphne, did not take apple pie or bean salad.

Chart for Problem 6

	Daphne	Lisa	Moira	Norma	Creighton	Farmer	Garson	Ordway	apple pie	bean salad	iced tea	potato salad
Brad												
Edward												
Homer												
Ken												
Creighton												
Farmer												
Garson												
Ordway												
apple pie												
bean salad												
iced tea												
potato salad												

7.   Money for Charities

Burke, Irvin, Pamela, and Samantha, whose last names are Easley, Freeman, Linton, and Ohmer, collected funds in different ways (carnival, door-to-door collections, newspaper drive, roller skating marathon) for different charities (American Cancer Society, March of Dimes, United Foundation, World Literature Crusade).

Match up everything from the clues below.

1. The boy who organized the newspaper drive did not collect for the United Foundation.

2. Samantha and Easley, whose projects occurred at different times, helped each other raise money.

3. The person who raised money for World Literature Crusade hasn't met Ohmer, but she has met Linton.

4. Irvin, who held a carnival to raise money, has met Samantha and Freeman, but he hasn't met the person who raised money by door-to-door collections.

5. Money for the American Cancer Society was not collected by a newspaper drive or a carnival.

Chart for Problem 7

	Easley	Freeman	Linton	Ohmer	American Cancer Society	March of Dimes	United Foun-dation	World Literature Crusade	carnival	door-to-door collection	news-paper drive	roller skating marathon
Burke												
Irvin												
Pamela												
Samantha												
American Cancer Society												
March of Dimes												
United Foun-dation												
World Literature Crusade												
carnival												
door-to-door collection												
news-paper drive												
roller skating marathon												

8.   Who Works for Whom?

Cass, Edward, Helen, and Joan, whose last names are Kline, Lincoln, MacLeod, and Neale, have jobs (executive secretary, file clerk, stenographer, typist) working for Adams, Brown, Drake, and Garner.

From the clues below, match up everything.

1. Kline, who has been at her job for only six months, is not the stenographer.

2. Neale, who doesn't work for Adams, and Cass, who doesn't work for Garner, are almost the same age.

3. The executive secretary, who has been working for Brown for three years, is five years older than Neale.

4. The typist's boss, who is not Garner, handed him a pile of work to do at the last minute yesterday.

5. Cass has been helping others all week, since his boss is on vacation until next Wednesday.

6. Joan, who doesn't work for Garner, is not MacLeod.

Chart for Problem 8

	Kline	Lincoln	MacLeod	Neale	executive secretary	file clerk	steno-grapher	typist	Adams	Brown	Drake	Garner
Cass												
Edward												
Helen												
Joan												
executive secretary												
file clerk												
steno-grapher												
typist												
Adams												
Brown												
Drake												
Garner												

9. Ages of Five

Five children (Alfred, Helena, Lester, Margaret, Ronald) were born on the same date (month and day) but not in the same year. The oldest is 10.

Find each person's age.

1. The younger girl is two years older than the youngest boy.

2. The 10 year old, who is Alfred's brother or sister, has a dog named Ginger.

3. The 4 year old, who is an only child, is 5 years younger than Margaret, and he has a cat named Tiger.

4. Nobody is one or six years old.

5. Lester is not the oldest boy.

Chart for Problem 9

					10
Alfred					
Helena					
Lester					
Margaret					
Ronald					

10. What Makes Cars Go

Alan, Betty, John, and Mary Ann, whose last names are Ferguson, Horton, Kelly, and Laramie, own a Camel, an Ostrich, a Panther, and a Tiger, which are cars which run on diesel fuel, electric power, gasohol, and solar energy.

Match everything up from the clues below.

1. Betty and Laramie asked the owner of the car powered by solar energy whether or not her car runs well on shady days.

2. Ferguson's car and the Panther have to stop at filling stations to refuel.

3. Neither the Tiger nor the car which uses gasohol is owned by John.

4. On cold days, Ferguson has trouble starting her car, which is not the Ostrich.

5. Horton, who does not own the Tiger or the Ostrich, has nicknamed her car "Spot."

6. The car owned by John, who is not Laramie, does not use diesel fuel.

Chart for Problem 10

	Ferguson	Horton	Kelly	Laramie	diesel fuel	electric power	gasohol	solar energy	Camel	Ostrich	Panther	Tiger
Alan												
Betty												
John												
Mary Ann												
diesel fuel												
electric power												
gasohol												
solar energy												
Camel												
Ostrich												
Panther												
Tiger												

11. Coats and Shoes

Agatha, Drake, Edward, and Greta bought coats in different patterns (checkered, flowered, plaid, striped) and different overall colors (gray, maroon, red, yellow). They also bought footwear (boots, house slippers, oxfords, tennis shoes).

Match up everything from the clues below.

1. The person who bought the boots, who did not buy the flowered coat, went to three stores before finding a pair of boots she liked.

2. Drake and the person who bought the flowered coat told the person who bought the yellow coat that they like his new shoes.

3. The person who bought the maroon coat did not buy the checkered coat or the boots.

4. The person who bought the striped coat told Edward, who didn't buy the checkered coat, that Edward's new kitten is nice.

5. Neither of the girls bought house slippers.

6. Agatha told the person who bought the oxfords and the red coat that the department store is having another sale next week.

Chart for Problem 11

	checkered	flowered	plaid	striped	gray	maroon	red	yellow	boots	house slippers	oxfords	tennis shoes
Agatha												
Drake												
Edward												
Greta												
gray												
maroon												
red												
yellow												
boots												
house slippers												
oxfords												
tennis shoes												

12. Household Chores

Four girls (Amanda, Beatrice, Vera, Wilma) did chores at home (clean the garage, mow the lawn, pull weeds, sweep the basement). Each girl has a sister (Kitty, Lottie, Ronnie, Tammy). The girls' last names are Dryden, Fraser, Howard, and Jamison.

From the clues below, match up everything.

1 . Amanda's sister helped Amanda do her chore.

2. Vera and her sister, who is not Tammy, helped Wilma with her job when they finished at their own house.

3. Wilma, who isn't Dryden, didn't sweep the basement.

4. Neither Vera nor Kitty's sister got stained hands, but the girls who pulled weeds did.

5. Neither Wilma nor Jamison is Tammy's sister.

6. Lottie didn't help with any of the chores, but her sister, who isn't Wilma and who didn't sweep the basement, didn't mind.

7. Howard, who is not Kitty's sister, did not pull weeds or clean the garage.

8. Howard, who isn't Amanda, was too tired to do anything but soak in the bathtub when she finished her chore.

Chart for Problem 12

	Dryden	Fraser	Howard	Jamison	Kitty	Lottie	Ronnie	Tammy	clean the garage	mow the lawn	pull weeds	sweep the basement
Amanda												
Beatrice												
Vera												
Wilma												
Kitty												
Lottie												
Ronnie												
Tammy												
clean the garage												
mow the lawn												
pull weeds												
sweep the basement												

13. Four at Dinner

A dentist, a nurse, a physician, and a veterinarian went to dinner together. Their names are Martin, Nelson, Owens, and Patrick. Assume traditional dating patterns.

Figure out who is what.

1. Owens asked Nelson and the nurse for dates but was turned down by both.

2. Patrick sat next to the dentist and across from the physician.

3. The men sat across the table from each other, as did the women.

4. Martin and the veterinarian are of opposite sex.

Chart for Problem 13

	dentist	nurse	physician	veterinarian
Martin				
Nelson				
Owens				
Patrick				

14. Favorite Drinks

Bernard, Dorothy, Edwin, Faith, and Jeannine, whose last names are Casey, Gardner, Hooper, Kulper, and Martin, have favorite drinks for hot weather (apple juice, iced tea, lemonade, orange juice, pineapple juice).

Match up the names and drinks from the clues below.

1. Hooper doesn't like apple juice.

2. Gardner doesn't like lemonade.

3. The person whose favorite is orange juice, who isn't Dorothy, gets along well with everyone.

4. Jeannine likes all the drinks, but she likes one, which isn't iced tea or orange juice, the best.

5. Edwin and Martin don't get along well with the person whose favorite is lemonade, who isn't Casey.

6. Martin and Jeannine and the person whose favorite is apple juice are good friends.

7. Aside from one other person, Bernard doesn't get along well with anyone.

8. Casey doesn't like some of the drinks, but she likes at least two of them.

Chart for Problem 14

	Casey	Gardner	Hooper	Kulper	Martin	apple juice	iced tea	lemonade	orange juice	pineapple juice
Bernard										
Dorothy										
Edwin										
Faith										
Jeannine										
apple juice						
iced tea						
lemonade						
orange juice						
pineapple juice						

SOLUTIONS

GENERAL COMMENTS ABOUT SOLUTIONS

There is more than one way to approach the solution of most Mind Benders®. For example, if a problem has five clues, you might choose to apply clue 4 first and clue 2 second, while the solution here for that problem uses clue 3 first and clue 5 second. Since there is only one final answer to the problem, the order in which the clues are used does not affect the final answer.

In order to understand a solution here, it is necessary that you have a copy of the problem to refer to while you are reading the solution. Also, it is definitely suggested, particularly for the problems in the B and C series, that you write down the findings as you go through a solution in order to help keep track of the rationale. For example, suppose a problem uses first and last names and occupations of three people. Before you start reading the solution here, write down the first names, leaving space to fill in the last names and occupations:

Bernard

Catherine

Donald

Then this is what your notes will look like as you read through (part of) the detailed solution, "Smith is a man (2) but isn't Donald (4), so he is Bernard."

Bernard Smith

Catherine

Donald

"The TV repairer is a man (3) but isn't Smith (3), so he is Donald."

Bernard Smith

Catherine

Donald,   TV repairer

Notice in the above example that clue numbers are referred to in parentheses.

DETAILED SOLUTIONS

1.

STUDENT	TEACHER	PEN COLOR
Jim	Fenner	red
Mary	Corwin	blue
Stella	Ephraim	black
Tom	Dalton	green

Corwin and Ephraim are women (1). Mary isn't Ephraim (2, 3), so Stella is, and Mary is Corwin. The green pen user is male (2) but isn't Jim (2, 3), so he is Tom. Then Tom isn't Fenner (4), so Jim is, and Tom is Dalton. The user of the red pen is male (5), so he is Jim. Corwin doesn't use a black pen (4), so Ephraim does, and Corwin uses a blue pen.

2.

FIRST NAME	LAST NAME	WORK
Andrew	Norton	electrician
Betty	Robbins	carpenter
Donna	Taylor	plumber
Jerome	Otis	mason

Andrew and Otis are men (1), so Taylor is a woman (1). Taylor isn't Betty (2), so Taylor is Donna. Robbins is a woman (4), so she is Betty. Andrew isn't Otis (1), so Jerome is, and Andrew is Norton.

A mason wouldn't finish work on a brick house before one of the other three contractors even started working, so Donna Taylor is not the mason (1). She isn't the electrician (2) or the carpenter (5), so she is the plumber. Betty is not the electrician (2) or the mason (3), so she is the carpenter. A mason wouldn't finish working on a brick house before an electrician started, so Andrew is the electrician and Jerome Otis is the mason (1).

3.

FIRST NAME	LAST NAME	GIFT
Angela	Lansdowne	game
Carlotta	Durwood	book
Elias	Nardon	jigsaw puzzle
Harold	Forman	record album
Igor	Kramer	model airplane kit

The book was given by a girl (5), but not by Angela (5), so Carlotta gave the book. Then Angela gave Sharon the game (7). Durwood is a girl (3) but isn't Angela (3, game), so she is Carlotta. Nardon (3), Forman (4), and Kramer (5) are boys, so Angela is Lansdowne.

Igor is not Forman or Nardon (6), so he is Kramer, and he gave the model airplane kit (2). Elias didn't give the record album (1), so Harold gave it, and Elias gave the jigsaw puzzle. A record album isn't something which is "put together" (6), so Nardon is not Harold (6). Then Elias is Nardon, and Harold is Forman.

4.

FIRST NAME	LAST NAME	HAIR COLOR
Catherine	Inwell	auburn
Duane	Klinger	yellow
Elias	Lopez	red
Harmony	Mason	black
Jane	Fernandez	gray

Duane's hair is yellow (1). Lopez is a male (2) but isn't Duane (2, yellow hair), so he is Elias. Mason is a female with curly hair (1) and is not Jane (2) or Catherine (3, straight hair), so she is Harmony.

The person with auburn hair is female (4) but isn't Harmony (4) or Jane (6), so she is Catherine. The person with red hair isn't Harmony (5, Mason) or Jane (6), so Elias has red hair.

Fernandez isn't Catherine (4, auburn hair) or Duane (4), so Jane is Fernandez. Catherine isn't Klinger (3), so Duane is, and so Catherine is Inwell.

Mason doesn't have gray hair (5), so Fernandez does, and so Mason's hair is black.

5.

PARENT	LAST NAME	CHILD	STORY
Alice	Garner	Thomas	Beauty and the Beast
Carlos	Ellman	Isabelle	Snow White
Kathleen	Jarvis	Fernando	Hansel and Gretel
Paul	Dorman	Monica	Red Riding Hood

The men read to girls (1), so the women read to boys. Jarvis' child is not a girl (4), so Jarvis is a woman. She isn't Alice (2), so she is Kathleen. Garner is a woman (3) so she is Alice. The women read "Beauty and the Beast" and "Hansel and Gretel" to their children (2). Garner didn't read "Hansel and Gretel" (3), so Jarvis read this, and Garner read "Beauty and the Beast." Since "Beauty and the Beast" wasn't read to Fernando (7), it was read to Thomas, and Fernando was read "Hansel and Gretel."

Isabelle's parent is not Paul (5), so he is Carlos, and so Paul's child is Monica. Since Carlos didn't read "Red Riding Hood" (5, Isabelle), Paul read this to Monica, and Carlos read "Snow White." Then Carlos is not Dorman (6), so Paul is Dorman, and Carlos is Ellman.

6.

HUSBAND	WIFE	LAST NAME	FOOD
Brad	Lisa	Garson	potato salad
Edward	Moira	Creighton	iced tea
Homer	Daphne	Ordway	bean salad
Ken	Norma	Farmer	apple pie

Mr. Farmer, who went on a bicycle (3), is not Brad (1, car) or Homer or Edward (5), so he is Ken. Mrs. Farmer, who also went on a bicycle (3), is not Moira (2, motorcycle) or Lisa or Daphne (5), so she is Norma.

Brad, who went in a car (1), is not married to Moira (2, motorcycle) or Daphne (7), so he is married to Lisa. Then Brad and Lisa are not the Creightons (4, no car) or the Ordways (1), so they are the Garsons.

Ordway went in a car (1), but Edward didn't (6), so Edward isn't Ordway. Then Homer is Ordway, and Edward is Creighton. The Farmers went on bicycles (3), the Garsons (Brad and wife) and the Ordways went in a car (1), and the other couple, who are the Creightons, went on motorcycles (2). Then Edward Creighton is married to Moira (2), and Homer Ordway is married to Daphne.

The apple pie was not taken by the Ordways (1), the Creightons (6, Edward), or the Garsons (7, Brad), so the Farmers took it. Brad didn't take iced tea (1) or bean salad (7), so he took potato salad. Edward didn't take the bean salad (6), so Homer took it, and Edward took the iced tea.

7.

FIRST	LAST	CHARITY	COLLECTION METHOD
Burke	Freeman	March of Dimes	newspaper drive
Irvin	Ohmer	United Foundation	carnival
Pamela	Easley	World Literature Crusade	door-to-door
Samantha	Linton	American Cancer Society	roller skating marathon

The newspaper drive, organized by a male (1), did not raise any money for United Foundation (1), World Literature Crusade (3, female), or American Cancer Society (5), so it raised money for March of Dimes.

Irvin held a carnival (4), so the boy in clue 1 is Burke. Irvin's carnival didn't raise money for World Literature Crusade (3, female) or American Cancer Society (5), so it raised money for United Foundation.

Samantha didn't raise money by collecting door-to-door (4), so Pamela did, and Samantha raised money by organizing a roller skating marathon.

Freeman is not Irvin or Samantha (4) or Pamela (4, door-to-door), so he is Burke. The person who collected money for the World Literature Crusade isn't Ohmer or Linton (3), so she is Easley. Easley isn't Samantha (2), so she is Pamela. Then Samantha raised money for the American Cancer Society.

Pamela and Linton have met (3, World Literature Crusade), but Pamela and Irvin have not met (4, door-to-door), so Irvin is not Linton. Then Irvin is Ohmer, and Samantha is Linton.

8.

FIRST NAME	LAST NAME	JOB	BOSS
Cass	MacLeod	stenographer	Adams
Edward	Neale	typist	Drake
Helen	Kline	file clerk	Garner
Joan	Lincoln	executive secretary	Brown

The typist is male (4) but isn't Cass, since Cass's boss is on vacation (5), but the typist's boss is not on vacation (4). So the typist is Edward.

Garner isn't the boss of Cass (2), Edward (4, typist), or Joan (6), so Helen works for Garner.

Kline, a female (1), is not the stenographer (1). She also is not the executive secretary, who has been on the job for three years (3, 1). So she is the file clerk. Cass, who is almost the same age as Neale (2), is not the executive secretary (3) or the file clerk (1, Kline, a female), so he is the stenographer. Then the executive secretary, who works for Brown (3), is Joan or Helen. She isn't Helen (Garner), so she is Joan. Then Helen is the file clerk, which makes Helen's last name Kline.

Joan is not MacLeod (6) or Neale (3, executive secretary), so she is Lincoln. Cass isn't Neale (2), so he is MacLeod, and Edward is Neale. Neale doesn't work for Adams (2), so MacLeod does, and Neal works for Drake.

9.

NAME	AGE
Alfred	3
Helena	5
Lester	4
Margaret	9
Ronald	10

Margaret is 9 years old (3). She cannot be the younger girl, for then the youngest boy would be only 7 (1), whereas we know there is a 4 year old (3). So Margaret is the older girl. Then the 10 year old is a boy. He is not Alfred (2) or Lester (5), so he is Ronald.

The 4 year old is a boy (3). Since he is an only child (3), he is not Alfred (2), so he is Lester. If Lester is the youngest boy, then Helena is 6 years old (1), but nobody is 6 years old (4), so Lester is not the youngest. The youngest, a boy (1), then must be Alfred. He is not 2 years old, for then Helena would be 4 years old (1), the same age as Lester, which is not possible (first paragraph of problem). Alfred is not 1 year old (4), so he is 3 years old, which makes Helena five years old (1).

10.

FIRST NAME	LAST NAME	FUEL	CAR
Alan	Laramie	gasohol	Panther
Betty	Ferguson	diesel	Tiger
John	Kelly	electric	Ostrich
Mary Ann	Horton	solar energy	Camel

The owner of the solar-powered car is female (1) but isn't Betty (1), so she is Mary Ann. John doesn't own the car powered by diesel fuel (6) or gasohol (3), so he owns the electric car. Then John, the electric car owner, doesn't have to stop at filling stations to refuel, so he is not Ferguson (2). Also, he isn't Horton (5, female) or Laramie (6), so he is Kelly.

Mary Ann, who owns the solar powered car, is not Laramie (1) or Ferguson (2), so she is Horton. Since the Panther is not powered by solar energy (2), Mary Ann Horton doesn't own the Panther, nor does she own the Tiger or the Ostrich (5). So she owns the Camel.

Alan is not Ferguson (4, female), so he is Laramie, and Betty is Ferguson. Ferguson doesn't own the Ostrich (4) or the Panther (2), so she owns the Tiger. Betty's Tiger is not powered by gasohol (3), so it uses diesel fuel. Then Alan's car uses gasohol and is, therefore, the Panther (2). Then John's car is the Ostrich.

11.

NAME	COAT PATTERN	COAT COLOR	FOOTWEAR
Agatha	checkered	gray	boots
Drake	striped	maroon	house slippers
Edward	plaid	yellow	tennis shoes
Greta	flowered	red	oxfords

The buyer of the yellow coat is male (2) but isn't Drake (2), so he is Edward. Edward didn't buy the house slippers (2, yellow coat) or the boots (1, female), or the oxfords (6, red coat), so he bought the tennis shoes.

One of the boys bought the house slippers (5), so this person has to be Drake. Agatha didn't buy the oxfords (6), so she bought the boots, and so Greta bought the oxfords and the red coat (6).

The flowered coat was not bought by Drake (2) or Edward (2, yellow coat) or Agatha (1, boots), so Greta bought it. Agatha didn't buy the maroon coat (3, boots), so she bought the gray coat, and Drake bought the maroon coat. Drake didn't buy the checkered coat (3, maroon), and neither did Edward (4), so Agatha bought it. Edward didn't buy the striped coat (4), so Drake bought it, and Edward bought the plaid coat.

12.

FIRST NAME	LAST NAME	SISTER	CHORE
Amanda	Dryden	Tammy	pulled weeds
Beatrice	Howard	Lottie	mowed lawn
Vera	Jamison	Ronnie	swept the basement
Wilma	Fraser	Kitty	cleaned the garage

Amanda's sister (1) and Vera's sister (2) helped with the chores, but Lottie didn't (6). Then Lottie's sister is not Amanda or Vera, and she is not Wilma (6), so Lottie's sister is Beatrice. Tammy's sister isn't Vera (2) or Wilma

(5), so she is Amanda. Kitty is not Vera's sister (4), so she is Wilma's sister, and Ronnie is Vera's sister.

Vera helped someone else when she was through with her own chore (2), but Howard didn't (8), so Howard is not Vera. Howard isn't Wilma (7, Kitty's sister) or Amanda (8), so she is Beatrice. Jamison is not Wilma (5) or Amanda (5, Tammy's sister), so she is Vera. Wilma isn't Dryden (3), so Amanda is, and Wilma is Fraser.

The person who pulled weeds is not Beatrice (7, Howard) or Vera (4) or Wilma (4, Kitty's sister), so she is Amanda. Neither Beatrice (6, Lottie's sister) nor Wilma (3) swept the basement, so Vera did. Beatrice didn't clean the garage (7, Howard), so Wilma did, and Beatrice mowed the lawn.

13.

NAME	JOB
Martin	nurse
Nelson	dentist
Owens	physician
Patrick	veterinarian

Nelson and the nurse are the same sex (1, since Owens asked both for dates), and Patrick and the physician are the same sex (2, 3). These are not just two people (Nelson = physician, Patrick = nurse), for then there would be only two people left, both of the same sex, and those would include Martin and the veterinarian, who are of opposite sex (4).

Then Nelson and the nurse are of one sex, while Patrick and the physician are of the other sex. Then Owens, who asked Nelson for a date (1), is the physician. And then Martin, the only last name not accounted for yet in the first sentence of the first paragraph, is the nurse. Patrick is not the dentist (2), so Nelson is, and Patrick is the veterinarian.

14.

FIRST NAME	LAST NAME	DRINK
Bernard	Hooper	lemonade
Dorothy	Martin	iced tea
Edwin	Gardner	apple juice
Faith	Casey	orange juice
Jeannine	Kulper	pineapple juice

Jeannine likes all the drinks (4), so she isn't Hooper (1), Gardner (2), or Casey (8). Also, she isn't Martin (6), so Jeannine is Kulper. Since Martin doesn't get along well with the person whose favorite is lemonade (5), but Martin is a good friend of Jeannine (6), Jeannine's favorite is not lemonade. Also, her favorite drink is not iced tea or orange juice (4) or apple juice (6), so it is pineapple juice.

The orange juice drinker, who gets along with everyone (3), isn't Bernard (7) or Edwin (5) or Dorothy (3), so she is Faith.

Martin doesn't get along well with the lemonade drinker (5), but the orange juice drinker gets along well with everyone (3), so Martin doesn't drink orange juice. Martin doesn't drink lemonade (5) or apple juice (6), so he or she drinks iced tea. The lemonade drinker is not Casey (5) or Gardner (2), so she or he is Hooper.

Martin gets along well with at least two people (6) but Bernard doesn't (7), so Martin is not Bernard. Martin isn't Faith (orange juice) or Edwin (5), so Martin is Dorothy. Casey is female (8), so she is Faith.

Edwin is not the lemonade drinker (5), so he isn't Hooper. Then Bernard is Hooper, and Edwin is Gardner and drinks apple juice.